Contents

 Where you see this symbol - adult supervision is required.

KT-393-857

Get ready to cook!

Cooking is a really good hobby. It's creative, it's fun – and you can eat the end result! It is also a great way of discovering different tastes and flavours, and what you do and don't like.

Oven mitts at the ready!

This book is about hot food that requires cooking in a pan on a hob, on a tray under a grill, in an ovenproof dish or tin in an oven, and in microwave-safe dishes in a microwave. Hot food is also about eating the food freshly cooked while still warm or hot from the oven or pan. Because these recipes involve cooking appliances and handling hot dishes and pans, an adult should be close by in the kitchen when you are cooking and oven gloves should always be ready to use!

 Where you see this symbol –
adult supervision is required.

Hot tips for a healthy you!

Food is really important – it gives you the energy to do all the things you love to do.

Food is fuel for your body. It keeps you moving and provides the energy for your growth and development. The best way to keep yourself healthy is to eat lots of different types of food so that you take in lots of different vital vitamins and nutrients.

You won't be healthy or happy if you eat only cake, or if you just eat carrots. One might make you fat; the other might, after a long time, turn you orange! But together, with a variety of other foods, they will keep you healthy and happy.

'Treats to Make and Bake' is brimming with recipes that are easy to prepare and cook, use lots of simple ingredients, and better still, taste and look great! But before you get started, read the 'Top ten tips' (pages 30-31) to help you become an ace chef!

What you need:

4 wooden skewers

12 cherry tomatoes

salt and pepper

2 tablespoons olive oil

2 cloves garlic

8 thick slices French bread

150 grams soft creamy herb and garlic cheese

1 Preheat the grill to a medium heat.

2 Put the tomatoes into a plastic bowl with a little salt and pepper and the oil. Place garlic in a garlic press, squeeze and add the crushed garlic to the bowl. Stir so that the tomatoes are evenly covered with seasoning and oil. Thread 3 tomatoes onto each wooden skewer.

3 Place tomatoes and bread slices onto a grill pan. Toast the bread until lightly golden brown.

4 Ask an adult to put the grilled bread onto a chopping board. Spread cheese onto the un-toasted side of the bread.

5 Turn the grill to high and return the bread – cheese-side up – to the grill pan with the tomatoes. You can ask an adult to help you do this. Toast bread for 2 to 3 minutes, or until the cheese starts to brown and the tomatoes have softened and split.

Tasty toasties

What you need:

2 bread rolls

olive oil

8 tablespoons tomato passata or pasta sauce

1 large tomato

2 mushrooms or 1/4 green pepper

125 grams mozzarella cheese

salt and pepper

EXTRA TOPPING IDEAS: ham, salami, tuna, pineapple, courgette, ricotta cheese, olives or capers

1 Set the oven to 220°C or gas mark 7.

2 Lightly oil a baking sheet or tray. Cut rolls in half and place them, cut-side up, onto the baking sheet.

3 Spread passata evenly onto the bread. Cut the tomato and mushrooms or pepper into thin slices. Decorate the pizzas with slices of each.

4 Slice the cheese and arrange slices onto the bread so that the cheese covers the passata.

5 Sprinkle with salt and pepper and drizzle a little oil over each pizza.

6 Ask an adult to place the pizzas into the oven to bake for about 20 minutes and to check that the pizzas are cooked before removing them from the oven. Pizza pronto is great as a snack, but add a salad and you have a main meal.

pizza pronto

7

What you need:

1 tablespoon olive oil

1 onion, chopped

1 stick celery, chopped

1 carrot, chopped

500 grams ground beef or vegetarian mince

1 green pepper, chopped

400-gram can chopped tomatoes

1 garlic clove, crushed

1 teaspoon dried mixed herbs

salt and black pepper

200-300 grams dried spaghetti

Parmesan cheese

1 Put oil, onion, celery and carrot into a pan. Cover with a lid and cook for 10 minutes over a low heat to soften the vegetables. Stir once or twice.

2 Add the mince and turn the heat to high. Stir the mixture to evenly cook and brown the mince.

3 Add the green pepper, tomatoes, garlic, herbs and salt and pepper to the pan. Stir until the sauce bubbles, then turn the heat to low. Let the sauce cook gently for 30 minutes.

4 Boil a large saucepan of water and add a pinch of salt. Add the spaghetti (break spaghetti in half if it is too long) and stir once. Cook for 10 minutes until the pasta is just tender. Drain the pasta in a colander.

5 Place spaghetti onto plates, spoon over the sauce and scatter with grated cheese.

Spaghetti special

What you need:

FILLING:

250 millilitres milk

50 grams butter

4 tablespoons flour

200 grams mushrooms, sliced or 100 grams ham, chopped

salt and pepper

PANCAKE BATTER:

250 millilitres milk

1 large egg

100 grams plain flour

vegetable oil

grated cheese

1. Set the oven to 200°C or gas mark 6.

2. Filling: place milk, butter and flour in a pan. Place on a medium heat and stir continuously until the milk has bubbled and thickened into a sauce. Take the pan off the heat and stir in the mushrooms or ham. Season with salt and pepper.

3. Pancake batter: blend milk, egg and flour together, or beat with a rotary beater gradually adding the milk. No lumps are allowed in a pancake batter!

4. Ask an adult to help with this stage. Heat a non-stick frying pan until very hot. Add a teaspoon of oil and tilt the pan so that oil covers the base. Add enough batter to thinly cover the pan. Fry for 1 to 2 minutes, until the bottom of the pancake is golden brown. Flip the pancake and let it cook for 1 minute. Tip it out onto kitchen paper. Repeat to make 6 to 8 pancakes.

5. Divide filling between the pancakes. Roll the pancakes and place in a buttered ovenproof dish. Sprinkle over cheese and bake for 15 to 20 minutes.

10

Pancake pillows

What you need:

500 grams mixed vegetables (carrot, pepper, spring onions, broccoli, mushrooms or leek), washed

250 grams cooked skinless chicken or tofu fillets, cooked

2 tablespoons vegetable oil

2 cloves garlic, peeled and crushed

125 grams beansprouts

150 millilitres stir-fry sauce

1 Peel and cut vegetables into fine slices, except broccoli, which should be cut into small pieces (florets).

2 Tear or cut chicken or vegetarian fillets into bite-size pieces.

3 Ask an adult to help with this stage. Heat a wok or large frying pan until it is very hot and then add the oil. Carefully add the chicken or tofu – stand back in case it spatters – then stir-fry while it cooks for 2 minutes and starts to brown.

4 Add the sliced vegetables and garlic. Stir-fry for 5 minutes.

5 Add the beansprouts and sauce and cook following the directions for the sauce.

6 Pile onto plates and get stuck in immediately to enjoy the stir-fry while it is crunchy and crispy!

Crispy, crunchy stir-fry

What you need:

2 large baking potatoes, washed and scrubbed clean

25 grams butter

100 grams grated cheese

100 grams ham, cut into squares (optional)

100 grams cooked peas or beans

salt and pepper

potato pockets

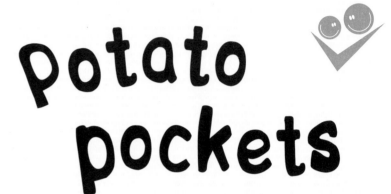

1 Set the oven to 220°C or gas mark 7.

2 Cut through the skin around the middle of both potatoes with a knife. This will stop the potatoes bursting in the oven! Place potatoes on a wire shelf in the oven and cook for 1 to $1^1/_4$ hours. Ask an adult to test if the potatoes are soft all the way through.

3 Wearing oven gloves, remove potatoes from the oven. Leave to cool slightly, then cut the potatoes in half and scoop out the soft white potato without breaking the skins. Put the skins on the baking sheet.

4 Put the potato in a bowl with the butter and mash it with a fork until smooth. Add half the cheese with the ham, peas or beans, and salt and pepper and mix again.

5 Spoon the potato filling back into the skins. Sprinkle over the remaining cheese and bake for 20 minutes until the cheese has browned.

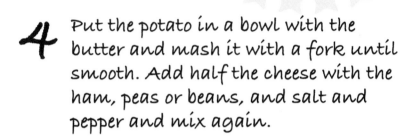

Sticky, swee**t** spicy pork

What you need:

1 pork fillet (about 500 grams)

SAUCE:
150-millilitre can cola

3 tablespoons clear honey

3 tablespoons red jam (like strawberry) without bits

3 tablespoons tomato ketchup

2 teaspoons French mustard

SERVE WITH: medium egg noodles, baby corn, bean sprouts and soy sauce

1 Set the oven to 220°C or gas mark 7.

2 Slice the pork thinly and place into a shallow baking tin lined with cooking foil.

3 Ask an adult to help cook the sauce. Put the sauce ingredients into a saucepan and mix together. Heat until the jam is melted, then boil for 10 minutes until the sauce has thickened a little. Stir well.

4 Pour the sauce over the pork making sure that every slice is well covered. Spread the pork out in the tin.

5 Ask an adult to place the tin in the oven for 30 minutes and to stir the mixture once or twice while it is roasting.

6 Just before the meat is ready, simmer the noodles and baby corn for 4 minutes. Drain and place onto a serving plate. Stir in bean sprouts and shake on soy sauce.

7 Ask an adult to remove the tin from the oven and to spoon the pork fillets onto the bed of noodles.

What you need:

350 grams cooked mixed vegetables, fresh or frozen

150 grams cooked potatoes

2 tablespoons olive oil

2 medium tomatoes

6 large eggs

salt and pepper

1 teaspoon dried mixed herbs

1/2 teaspoon paprika

75 grams grated cheese

1 Set the oven to 190°C or gas mark 5.

2 Chop the cooked vegetables into 2.5-centimetre dice, and the potatoes into 1-centimetre dice. If you are using frozen mixed vegetables, follow the directions on the packet.

3 Pour the oil into a baking dish, add the chopped vegetables and potatoes and stir well. Ask an adult to put the dish into the oven to bake for 10 minutes.

4 Cut the tomatoes into chunks, and leave them to one side.

5 Beat the eggs with the salt, pepper, herbs and paprika in a bowl.

6 Ask an adult to remove the dish from the oven and to place it on a pot stand. Stir in the tomatoes, then the eggs and stir well. Scatter the cheese on top.

7 Ask an adult to put the dish back into the oven to bake for 30 minutes or until the eggs are set and the cheese melted. Cut into wedges and serve as a hearty winter meal with steamed vegetables.

Veggie cheese bake

What you need:

1 orange, peeled

1 large banana, peeled

15 seedless green grapes

1 tablespoon desiccated coconut

100 grams chocolate, chopped into small chunks

25 grams unsalted butter

8 sheets filo pastry

icing sugar

1 Set the oven to 200°C or gas mark 6.

2 Break the orange into segments and cut into smaller pieces. Cut the banana into slices. Place both fruits in a bowl. Mix in the grapes, coconut and chocolate.

3 Melt the butter in a small pan on the hob or in a dish in the microwave.

4 Place 4 filo sheets on the worktop, with short sides nearest you. Brush each sheet with a little melted butter. Lay another sheet of filo onto the buttered sheet and brush with melted butter.

5 Spoon the fruit mixture evenly along one short edge of each filo stack. Leave space at the ends. Fold the long sides in and brush with butter. Roll the filo stacks to make 4 sausage-shaped strudels.

6 Butter a baking tray, place the strudels on it and brush with the remaining melted butter. Ask an adult to place the tray into the oven to bake for 10 minutes.

7 Allow the strudels to cool a little, then sprinkle with icing sugar.

Chocolate fruit strudels

What you need:

40 grams butter, cut into slivers

4 eating apples

1/2 lemon

10 ready-to-eat dried apricots

3 tablespoons seedless raisins

2 tablespoons soft, light brown (muscovado) sugar

100 millilitres orange juice

1 Set the oven to 200°C or gas mark 6.

2 Lightly butter a baking dish with a little of the butter.

3 Cut the apples in half across the core and scoop out seeds with a teaspoon. Rub the cut apple with lemon and put the apples, cut side up, in the dish.

4 Cut each apricot into 3, then mix them in a bowl with the raisins, remaining butter and sugar. Spoon the mixture evenly onto each apple and pour the orange juice over.

5 Place baking paper over the fruit to stop the raisins burning. Ask an adult to place the baking dish into the oven to bake for 30 minutes, or until the apples are tender.

6 Serve the apple splits with the sweet, buttery juice from the baking dish spooned over.

hot apple splits

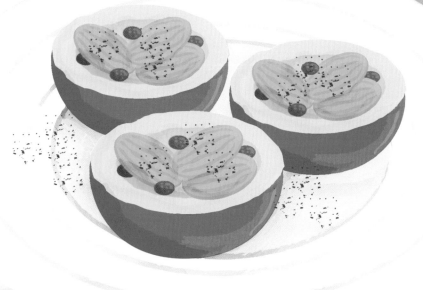

What you need:

750 grams cooking apples

Juice of 1/2 lemon

4 tablespoons water

100 grams sugar

200 grams plain flour

100 grams butter, cut into small chunks

100 grams raw sugar (demerara)

50 grams walnut or pecan pieces

Nuts about crumble

1. Set the oven to 200°C or gas mark 6. Lightly butter a baking dish.

2. Cut the apples into quarters and peel each quarter. Cut away the core and then slice the fruit into a saucepan.

3. Add the lemon juice, water and sugar and cook over a medium heat for about 10 minutes, until the apples have become very soft. Stir, then spoon the apple mixture into the baking dish to cool slightly.

4 Put the flour and butter into a mixing bowl. Rub the butter into the flour between your fingers and thumbs until the mixture looks like biscuit crumbs.

5 Stir in the sugar and nuts.

6 Tip the crumble into the dish over the apple and smooth it down gently.

7 Ask an adult to place the baking dish into the oven to bake for 30 minutes, until the topping is brown. Let the crumble cool a little before spooning onto plates and serving with cream, custard or ice cream.

What you need:

25-centimetre baking dish

40 grams butter

500 grams cherries, fresh or frozen and defrosted, and stones removed

3 large eggs

3 tablespoons plain flour

pinch of salt

5 tablespoons caster sugar

450 millilitres milk

1 Set the oven to 200°C or gas mark 6.

2 Grease the baking dish with a little butter. Place the cherries in the dish.

3 Use a whisk or wooden spoon to beat the eggs, flour, salt and 3 tablespoons of the sugar in a bowl until smooth.

4 Heat the milk until almost boiling – it will start to steam gently when it is ready. Pour the milk over the egg mixture and mix until smooth.

5 Pour the egg and milk mixture over the cherries. Cut the remaining butter into slivers and scatter them over the pudding.

6 Ask an adult to help with this stage. Place the baking dish into a roasting tin. Carefully pour warm water into the roasting tin to come half-way up the sides of the baking dish. Place the dishes into the oven for 35 to 40 minutes, until the batter is set like a custard and lightly golden. Sprinkle with the remaining sugar and serve warm.

Cherry, cherry

What you need:

25-centimetre baking dish

PUDDING: 2 bananas sliced

150 grams self-raising flour

2 tablespoons cocoa powder

150 grams soft baking margarine

150 grams caster sugar

2 large eggs, beaten

2 tablespoons milk

SAUCE: 100 grams caster sugar

150 millilitres water

50 grams drinking chocolate

1 Set the oven to 190°C or gas mark 5. Lightly butter a baking dish and cover the base with banana slices.

2 Sift the flour and cocoa into a bowl. Add all the other pudding ingredients and stir well with a wooden spoon. Spoon the mixture evenly over the bananas.

3 Ask an adult to place the dish in the oven to cook for 40 minutes and to test if the pudding is cooked by pressing the top gently with his/her fingers. If the pudding springs back, it is ready to eat!

4 To make the sauce: put the sugar and water in a pan. Stir over a low heat until the sugar has dissolved.

5 Turn up the heat and let the mixture boil for 1 minute, then add the chocolate. Take the pan off the heat and whisk hard to make a smooth sauce.

6 Serve pudding onto plates and smother with warm sauce.

Double chocolate treat

Top ten tips for

1 Enjoy yourself!

2 Get into washing your hands big time. Wash your hands when you start preparing food and during the cooking when hands have become sticky or you have been handling uncooked fish or meat. Make sure everything you use – dishes, bowls, tools and cutting boards, for example – are also clean.

3 Wear an apron to protect your clothes and to look like an ace chef. An apron is also the perfect thing for dabbing away sticky messes from fingertips!

4 Top chefs get all the ingredients prepared and chopped before they start cooking. They do this as a double-check that they have everything and so that they can concentrate on the creative bit – the cooking.

5 Clear up as you go. This means that you will be able to enjoy what you have prepared as soon as

budding chefs!

it is ready. It is very boring to be washing up while pizza waits to be eaten.

6 Sharp knives are safe if used with great care. Always ask an adult to help you. Hold a knife by its handle, blade pointing down, and carry it at your side.

7 When using pans on the hob, handles must be turned inward.

8 Never leave knives or dangerous kitchen tools, hot pots or uncooked foods within reach of younger children.

9 Always ask an adult to help you and use oven gloves when handling pans from the hob or dishes and tins from the oven or microwave.

10 You must always ask an adult for permission to use the kitchen. In return, the adult will be on hand to help with hot pans and dishes, to check if a mixture or ingredient is fully cooked and, maybe even, to do some of the washing up!

Recipes and accompanying text: Rosemary Moon

Cover and content illustrations: Sarah Wade

The information in this book has been thoroughly researched and checked for accuracy, and safety advice is given where appropriate. Neither the author nor the publisher can accept any responsibility for any loss, injury or damage incurred as a result of using this book.

An adult should supervise a child when he or she is cooking in the kitchen.

Published by Autumn Publishing,
A division of Bonnier Media Ltd.,
Chichester, West Sussex, PO20 7EQ, UK.

© 2011 Autumn Publishing

Printed in China